GROWING UP...
AND GRIEVING
Coping with Loss and Change

Marge Eaton Heegaard

Woodland Press
Minneapolis MN

GROWING UP...AND GRIEVING:
Coping With Loss and Change

Marge Eaton Heegaard. Original title,
COPING WITH DEATH & GRIEF
by Marge Eaton Heegaard,
Copyright O 1990 Lerner Publications
ISBN 0-8225-0043-4 (lib. bdg.)

Revised 2016 by Marge Eaton
Heegaard with permission
from Lerner Publications CO.

ISBN 978-0-9966390-1-9
Printed in the United States of America
Cover & inside illustrations by Hetty Mitchell

WOODLAND PRESS
952-830-9423
marheeg@me.com

ACKNOWLEDGEMENT FOR
PREVIOUS PUBLISHED WORK
"THINKING" by Joanna Redman, printed with
permission.."FEELING PERSON EXERCISE"
from WHEN SOMEONE VERY SPECIAL DIES by
Marge Eaton Heegaard, "EXPRESSING ANGER"
And "GUIDELINES FOR CREATIVE GRIEF WORK"
from GRIEF: A Natural Reaction To Loss
by Marge Eaton Heegaard

TO MY SONS
JIM, JON AND MICHAEL EATON
aged 9, 10 and 12 when their father
died...and will work to keep my books
available to grieving children when I
am unable to.

With special thanks to the many young people who
have shared their experiences and feelings of grief
with me, and to my editor, LeeAnne Engfer, for her
helpful suggestions and support.

Contents

1 Living Means Changing 7

2 Death Is the End of Living 13

3 Saying Goodbye Is Difficult 19

4 Feeling Terrible 27

5 Letting out Your Feelings 35

6 When a Family Member Dies 41

7 When Someone Else Is Grieving . . 47

8 Feeling Good about You 52

  Glossary 60

  Index 61

LIFE BRINGS MANY CHANGES.   PLEASE LIST THE CHANGES YOU HAVE ALREADY EXPERIENCED:

(YOUR AGE AT TIME)

_____MOVE TO A NEW HOME

_____MOVE TO A NEW SCHOOL

_____GOOD FRIEND MOVED AWAY

_____LOSS OF A PET

_____PERSONAL SERIOUS ILLNESS

_____SERIOUS ILLNESS IN YOUR FAMILY

_____DEATH OF A FRIEND

_____DEATH OF A FAMILY MEMBER

      _____PARENT
      _____SIBLING
      _____GRANDPARENT

      OTHER _____

OTHER SIGNIFICNT CHANGES (please specify)

1
Living Means Changing

Julie recognized the large white house on the corner as the school bus slowed down. She felt a pang in her stomach when she looked at the house next to the white one.

"That is where I live now," she reminded herself, "but it doesn't seem like home!" Her family had moved last month, and her new city still seemed like a sea of strange faces and houses. She picked up her backpack and waited while others pushed into line and squeezed out the door. A cold gust of wind dared her to come out.

"I don't care how cold it is...I'd rather walk to school the way I did before!" Julie thought. She wondered how it was possible to feel so lonely in a crowd.

"Call me when you get home, Tom," a freckle-faced boy said to his friend as he left the bus. "Maybe we can go skating."

7

Everyone seemed to be in a hurry to get home. Julie was not in a hurry, but she was glad to be out of school. It was hard for her to keep her mind on her schoolwork. She kept thinking about how different everything was from her old school. She couldn't get her work finished and had to bring it home.

"Everyone will think I'm dumb," she worried. "And my grades will be terrible." She turned up her collar against the cold and looked down the street. Two girls were walking ahead of her, talking and laughing together. Julie thought of her friend Amy. She missed her so much. They had been best friends since kindergarten and had always walked to school together.

"I have great news," her stepfather had announced last summer. "I've been promoted, and we will be moving!" Mom had acted excited about moving, too.

"Great news," Julie thought, "it was the worst thing that ever happened to me!" She had to leave behind many things that were important to her.

"Nothing will ever take away this sadness," she thought. Her mother had told her that she would make friends in her new school, and her loneliness would end.

A girl named Becky seemed nice and had tried to be friendly, but Julie hadn't felt like being friendly today. She had smiled, though.

Julie wasn't smiling as she walked toward her house. "Hi Mom," she called when she entered the kitchen.

"Hi sweetie," Mom gave her a hug and then looked at her. "Did things go better today?"

"It was okay." Julie forced a smile. She picked up

her books. "I have a lot of homework." Julie went to her room, closed the door, and lay down on her bed. She didn't burst into tears as she had so many times before. She looked around her room. She was glad Mom had let her choose the color for her walls. The quilt Aunt Dee had made for Julie when she was little looked pretty hanging on the yellow wall.

"I'll write to Amy tonight and tell her about my new room," Julie promised herself. "She'll be happy to hear we're coming back to visit in April."

The telephone rang. "It's for you, Julie," Mom called.

"Hi Julie. This is Becky." Julie recognized her voice. "Lucy and I are going to work on our science project and we wondered if you would like to come over."

Julie's eyes brightened and she answered, smiling, "I'd really like that. I've noticed you getting off the bus, so I know where you live. I'll ride my bike over."

Facts about Change and Loss

Julie is having a hard time coping with moving from a small town to a larger city because of the many changes the move has created in her life. When families move, they cannot take everything with them. They have to leave people and things behind.

No one can avoid change. To grow means to change. You see change every day as days turn into nights. Weather changes. Seasons change. People change, too. Think about how much you have changed since you were born. You no longer look how you did in baby pictures.

Change can happen slowly or suddenly. Often you cannot control change. Changes can be good or they can be difficult. In many places, winter brings an end to outdoor swimming but marks the start of the ski season. Your favorite TV series may end, but a more exciting series might replace it. Usually when something changes, you notice first what you have lost.

Many kinds of losses

It is easy to recognize the loss of things you own. Items like clothes and toys wear out or get broken, lost, or stolen. You may give things away when you no longer need them. It is easier to give something away than to have it taken away.

Many losses are a natural part of growing older. Starting school, graduating from high school, going to college, getting married, becoming a parent, retiring, and aging are all events that create losses as well as gains. Family relationships and friendships may change because of death, divorce, moving, or disagreements.

Some losses are harder to recognize and understand. When something in your life changes, you may start to feel differently about yourself and others. Julie lost things and people that were important to her. There had been many changes in Julie's life since her mother remarried. Julie felt like she had no control over her life. She worried about what might happen next.

Healthy ways to cope with change and loss

What kinds of losses have you experienced? You may

still react to losses now in the same way you did when you lost something or someone important when you were little. You learned what you did and how you felt then from the adults around you.

Julie's family didn't talk much about feelings. Julie tried to put on a smile even though she felt sad. Her mother didn't realize how hard it was for her to move to a new city. Julie probably appeared unfriendly to many students at her new school. This made it more difficult for her to make new friends. Becky could understand the way Julie was acting because Becky had moved a few years before and remembered what it was like.

People react in different ways to the same kind of loss. Not everyone reacts to moving the way Julie did. Some people like change. Others try to avoid change. They may pretend nothing is different or try to replace what is lost. Some feel guilty because they think they caused the change. Most people feel some sadness and may or may not show it. It is natural to feel sad and angry when something or someone important to you is taken away.

When you experience a loss, it isn't healthy to pretend that nothing has changed and to keep your feelings inside. It is healthy to recognize what has been lost and what might be gained. It is healthy to let others know what you are feeling.

Remember that you cannot prevent some kinds of change. There will be difficult times in everyone's life. Learning to accept change and to deal with losses is part of growing up.

2
Death Is the End of Living

Brian jumped out of bed when he saw the sun streaming in his window.

"Great! It isn't raining, so we can work on our fort," he thought, pulling on his jeans. He carefully picked a shirt to wear. He didn't want his mother to send him back to his room to change. He had no time to waste! He had to get over to David's house.

"Is it all right if I go over to David's house this morning? We want to work on our fort," he asked his mother as he helped himself to some cereal in the kitchen.

"Not this morning, I'm afraid. You have your regular chores to do, and Dad has something he wants your help with." Brian's mother offered him some fruit.

Brian's smile turned into a frown. "I'll clean my room tonight. It won't take long. We *have* to work on our fort today! It rained last weekend."

"You'll have lots of time to work on that this summer. It can wait. Your room is a mess and so is Buffer's pen. That needs to be cleaned right now!" Brian knew by the way she sounded that nothing could change her mind.

"I was just going to feed him," Brian said, finishing his cereal. "That darn rabbit hutch always needs cleaning," he thought. He went into the garage and got a cup of rabbit food out of the bag. He remembered how hard it had been to talk his mother into getting a rabbit. He had promised to do all the work without complaining. It had turned out to be a lot more work than he expected, and most of it was pretty boring.

But Buffer was never boring. He was always so happy to see Brian when he came home from school.

"Something is wrong," Brian thought as he walked toward the hutch. Buffer usually heard him coming and stood up to greet him. The rabbit seemed to be asleep, but he was stretched out strangely.

"Oh, no!" Brian's heart skipped a beat. He reached in the pen for his pet. Buffer's body was stiff and hard. He wasn't soft and cuddly. His eyes were open, but glassy. Brian put the rabbit back down on the grass.

"Mom," he screeched. "Something has happened to Buffer!" Brian's mother heard the scream and hurried outside. Brian was staring down at his pet.

"Buffer's dead," he cried when he saw her. "Hurry up! Do something. Maybe he isn't really dead!"

"I'm afraid I can't fix him. He's dead, Brian." She hugged Brian to her. "I wish I could, but I can't."

"It's my fault," he sobbed. "I didn't take good care of

him. I should have cleaned his hutch more often." Brian's mother put her arm around him.

"These things happen," she said. "Rabbits don't live forever. Buffer didn't die because of anything you did or didn't do. You took good care of him. We'll take him to the vet, Brian. He can tell us why he died," she said as she wiped away a tear. She squeezed Brian's shoulder and they cried softly together.

Facts about Death

Brian feels like he caused his pet's death. Brian's mother wanted Brian to talk to the veterinarian so he could learn that it wasn't his fault that Buffer died. The death of a pet is many people's first experience with death. When your pet dies, you may have many questions that are difficult to answer. Many people are not comfortable talking about death. If you don't get answers, you might believe that it is not all right to talk about death. But it is important to be able to talk about death.

Death is part of life

All living things will die, including plants, animals, and human beings. Every living thing has a natural **life span**, or length of life. Dogs, cats, rabbits, and most other pets do not live as long as human beings.

Not every person lives a long life, either. Accidents happen, serious illnesses cannot always be cured, and people die. Medical advances have made it possible for most people to live longer than they did in the past.

Many people see death as something that does not have to happen. Yet death remains a part of life.

Most of the deaths you see in movies, TV, or newspapers are not realistic. Most deaths are not violent, and not all death is bad. It can mean the end of suffering for very old or very ill people. Most deaths happen in hospitals or nursing homes. Because death often happens away from home, it may seem mysterious or scary. It helps to learn more about death.

Physical facts about death

When someone dies, his or her body and brain stop working. Breathing stops, and the heart stops beating. Thinking, seeing, and feeling stop. The person's body temperature drops and the skin changes color. The muscles become stiff. Brain-wave tests, reflex-action tests, and tests to determine the reaction of the eye to light are used to prove death. A doctor records the time of death and the cause of death on a certificate. Veterinarians are doctors who treat animals. They can often figure out the cause of death of pets.

Causes of death

Maybe you are worried that something you did or didn't do caused your pet to die, but animals die for many reasons. Dogs and cats run into busy streets. Goldfish may come from the pet store with a disease.

It is easier to accept death when it comes to an old person or pet—someone or something at the end of the natural stages of life called the **life cycle**. Babies and children rarely die, because most illnesses can be prevented with vaccinations or treated with medications.

Accidents are one of the main causes of death for young people in the United States. Drugs and alcohol also kill some young people. The most common causes of death for older people are strokes, heart disease, heart attacks, and cancer. A **stroke** is the sudden loss of brain function, which happens when blood is blocked from reaching the brain. **Heart attacks** occur when the walls or arteries of the heart become plugged. **Cancer** is an uncontrolled growth of cells.

Some diseases are **congenital**, which means it is something you are born with. Some diseases are **hereditary**, which means the disease is something you inherit from a parent or grandparent.

Suicide

Some people end their own lives. There may be many different reasons for this. Some people feel hopeless and alone and want an immediate end to their emotional pain. When people commit suicide, it is especially painful for those they leave behind.

All life ends

Neither medicine nor good care can prolong life forever. You can't always protect someone from death. You can become less afraid of death by learning how to accept the sad as well as the happy parts of life.

People and animals you love will die. You will learn how to say a final goodbye.

FEELING PERSON EXERCISE

FEELINGS ARE SOMETHING YOU FEEL SOMEPLACE IN YOUR BODY. Close your eyes and think about a time when you felt really angry. Determine where in your body you feel anger. Scribble that area or areas with a red crayon. Do the same thing for your other feelings, using different colors for each feeling.

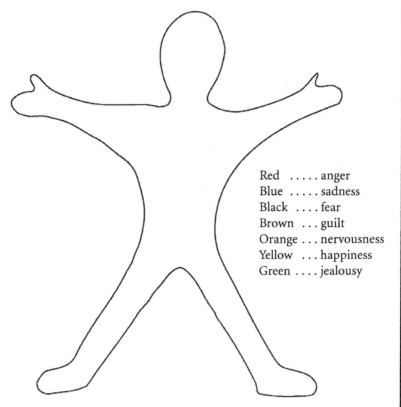

Red . . . . . anger
Blue . . . . . sadness
Black . . . . fear
Brown . . . guilt
Orange . . . nervousness
Yellow . . . happiness
Green . . . . jealousy

Feelings that are repressed often cause physical problems. Do you get aches and pains in the same places where you store anger, fear, or other feelings?

From *When Someone Very Special Dies* by Marge Eaton Heegaard, adapted with permission.

3
Saying Goodbye Is Difficult

Ann stopped brushing her hair. She held her breath, stood very still, and looked at herself in the mirror.

"What do dead people look like?" she wondered. Ann had seen dead "things" before. She remembered when she was about six and her bird died. She had held it. It wasn't sleeping, and it looked and felt different. It was stiff.

"It's dead, Ann," her brother had told her. She had cried and told her mother. They had wrapped it in some tissue and put it in a box and buried it. Ann had found some pretty stones and marked the grave.

She could smile now as she thought about the bird that had been her first pet. Gramma had given it to her. Ann stopped smiling.

"Gramma can never give me any more presents! I can't ever bake cookies with her again." Ann's stomach hurt when she thought about it. Gramma had died three days ago, and the funeral would be today.

"Maybe I'll get sick and have to stay home," she hoped. She had never been to a funeral. She was afraid to go. It didn't seem possible that her grandmother was dead.

"Her heart stopped," Mom had said. Ann put her hand over her own heart to make sure it was still working. At times it seemed to beat much too fast, and other times Ann couldn't feel it beating at all.

"You are too young to have a heart attack," Mom had said. "Gramma was old and had high blood pressure. Her heart hadn't worked well for years."

Ann thought about what she had learned about the heart in health class at school, and she felt better. Mom told her it was normal to worry about your own health for a while after someone else dies.

Ann didn't tell her mother that she also worried about her. Ann wondered what would happen now that Gramma wasn't around to help Mom out. Gramma had spent a lot of time with Ann and Mom ever since Mom and Dad got divorced, three years ago. Her mother had cried when she got the telephone call about Gramma, and she still looked sad and tired.

"Maybe that is normal, too," Ann hoped. She wanted to ask her mother about funerals, but Mom had been so busy planning the funeral that Ann hadn't had a chance to talk with her.

"I wish I had gone to the funeral last year when Paula's grampa died," Ann thought. "I would know what they do at funerals, and it would have been nice to have a best friend there." Paula hadn't talked much about the funeral afterwards, and Ann had been afraid to ask.

Ann's mom had told her that funerals are a way of saying goodbye to someone you care about.

"I don't want to say goodbye to Gramma!" Ann's eyes filled with tears.

"Could I talk with you for a few minutes, Ann?" her mother asked from outside Ann's bedroom door. Ann opened the door. "I have something for you," her mother said. "This was one of Gramma's prettiest handkerchiefs, and I think she would like you to have it to remember her by. She always said she liked to have a special hanky for special tears...and I think we may all have those today. Gramma was so special."

"Thanks, Mom," Ann said as she looked at the lace-edged white hanky with embroidered flowers.

"And now, Ann," Mom gave her a hug, "there are a few things I want to tell you about funerals...."

Facts about Funerals and Memorial Services

Funerals are a time for family and friends to say a formal goodbye to a loved one who has died. Gathering together helps each person know he or she is not alone. They can share their **grief**. Grief is the name for the many feelings you feel when you lose something or someone very important to you. As people remember a life that has ended, they often think about the meaning death gives to their lives.

People all over the world have different ways of mourning the end of life. In the United States, funerals and memorial services are most common.

When someone dies, friends and family must be informed and a funeral service must be planned. A funeral director and a minister, priest, or rabbi usually help plan a funeral or memorial service. A memorial service is similar to a funeral except there is no **casket** (box used to bury a dead person) at the service. The body may have been buried or **cremated** (reduced to ashes) before the service.

Cremation

When a body is cremated, it is reduced to ashes by intense heat, and the ashes are placed in an urn or a box. The ashes might be buried, scattered, or kept. Cremation may be chosen because it is less expensive and requires less burial space.

Preparing the dead for burial

Embalming is a process that replaces the blood in the **corpse** (dead body) with a fluid that will keep the body from decaying. After the body is embalmed, it feels cold and hard, like wax. The **mortician**, who prepares the body for burial, uses cosmetics to make the body look as the person did before death, but the body may still appear as it is—an empty shell of the person.

Viewing the dead

Reviewals or **wakes** are often held the night before

the funeral to let family and friends see the body before it is buried. For many people, the death may not seem real until then. Sometimes the coffin is not open but remains closed, with photographs of the person on it.

Friends come to the wake to offer support and comfort to the family of the dead person. Most people stay for just a short time. They often feel sad and don't know what to say to the family members. Families say that it helps just to have people come, because it shows they care. A look, touch, or hug can say more than words.

The funeral service

Often the funeral director and someone from the church or synagogue helps the family make plans for prayers and music. Someone may read verses from the Bible or Torah or other books. Several people may choose to talk about the person who died and what his or her life meant to them.

Many people cry at funerals. It is all right to cry when someone you love dies. You don't have to hide your feelings. Other people don't cry and that is all right, too. For some, the death may not seem real at first and tears come later. Others may be there because of their love for the family and not feel the deep sadness the family feels.

Memorials

Friends and relatives of the **deceased** (dead person) may send flowers to the church, synagogue, or funeral home as tokens of love and caring. Flowers and gifts of food or money are also sent to the grieving family's home. Money is often donated to a charity in honor of the one who died. Other kinds of memorials may be chosen as a special way to honor and remember the person.

Cemeteries

Cemeteries, or graveyards, are places where the dead are buried. People who work in cemeteries try to make the graves and the grounds around them a peaceful and pretty place for people to visit and think about the loved one who died. Some people feel pain and sadness at cemeteries and avoid them. Others find them comforting and enjoy bringing flowers to the grave on special days. Many people bring flowers to remember their dead on Memorial Day.

Graveside service

The final ritual is taking the casket to the cemetery, where a **grave** has been prepared. It is the last time to say goodbye and may be the most difficult. Sometimes only the family and close friends of the deceased attend the graveside service. If it is a military funeral, a bugle call which is called **taps** is played by an honor guard as a final salute.

A marker of marble, stone, or metal with the person's name and dates of birth and death will be placed at the grave. It is a mark of a life that will be remembered for many years by present and future generations.

After the service

After the funeral, many people may gather for refreshments. This can be a special reunion of relatives and friends, a time when they can find strength and comfort in each other. They will remind each other of happier times in the past, so there will be sounds of laughter among the sounds of sadness. Humor is not a sign of disrespect. It is healthy and natural to laugh when you are sad, just as people often cry on happy occasions like weddings.

Spiritual beliefs

Many people believe that everyone has a "soul" or "spirit," which are the qualities that make a person special. You cannot see the spirit. It is not like a heart or brain. It never gets sick and never wears out. When someone dies, the spirit leaves the body and no one knows for certain where it goes.

Faith means believing in something that you cannot see or prove. Many people around the world believe the spirit lives on. Some people believe the spirit goes to heaven to be with God. Others think the soul takes a new form after death, like the caterpillar that becomes a butterfly. Some people think the spirit becomes a part of those the person loved. There are other people who believe that there is nothing after death.

We don't know everything about life and death. We do know something about the feelings of grief that follow death, though.

EXPRESSING ANGER

EVERYONE GETS ANGRY at the loss of a loved one. Everyone. It is okay to feel anger toward the person who died; the person, illness, or situation that caused the death; and anything or anyone contributing to the death. It is not okay to hate yourself; threaten to harm yourself or others; or harm yourself, others, or things.

ACCEPTABLE WAYS TO EXPRESS ANGER

- Pause for a count of ten.
- Talk about it directly.
- Write it out, then tear up the angry thoughts or scribble them out with a red crayon.
- Exercise or play sports.
- Stomp (privately) or run.
- Engage in a throwing motion (i.e., play catch).
- Play an instrument.
- Yell in the shower or other private place.
- Punch a bag or pillow.

TECHNIQUES FOR SHARING YOUR ANGER WITH OTHERS

1) Decide what you are really angry about.
2) Release some anger in one of the ways suggested above.
3) Share your feelings with the person you are angry at (if possible and appropriate) or with a trusted other. Use "I" messages ("you" messages provoke defensiveness):

   I am angry because. . . .
   I feel. . . .
   I need/want. . . .

4) Listen carefully to the response and try to understand.
5) Make an appropriate response that does not escalate the situation.

4
Feeling Terrible

Mike watched his friends ride down the street on their bikes. He wanted to go with them, but they were biking to Mud Lake, and he knew his mother wouldn't let him go. He didn't even ask. She wouldn't let him do anything since his younger brother was killed. Bobby had been riding a bicycle when a car hit him. That was two months ago.

"I'm two years older than Bobby was," Mike thought as he watched his friends turn the corner. "I know how to take care of myself." Sometimes he felt angry at his brother. "He should have been more careful. He was always in a hurry."

The night before, Mike's father had shouted, "You can't expect a nine-year-old to watch for cars all the time. Drivers should watch out for kids." It seemed to Mike that his mom and dad got angry more often lately. Sometimes they got mad at each other. Other times they were angry with Mike.

"I should have been with Bobby," Mike thought. His face clouded over. "I would have seen that car. I could have told him to watch out." He remembered Bobby with his brown hair and freckles and how he was always fooling around. "I loved him...I really did," Mike kicked the ground with his foot as he remembered how his mother used to ask him to include his little brother in his activities. But there were times when Mike wanted to do things alone with his friends, without Bobby.

"I'll have plenty of time for that now," he thought. He closed his eyes tightly, trying to push the picture of Bobby out of his mind. He remembered too many times he had wished he didn't have a little brother. It hurt too much to think about that now.

"Hi, Mike." His little sister came out the door with her roller skates. "Do you want to skate with me?"

"I'm busy, Kristy," he lied. "Maybe later." Mike wondered how Kristy could act as if nothing terrible had happened. She always looked happy. She had cried only when she first heard about it. Mike wondered if she really understood that Bobby would never come back.

Mike went inside and turned on the television. He knew there wasn't anything good on, but he didn't want to think anymore. Dad would be home soon and maybe they could play catch.

"I doubt that," he frowned. They hadn't played catch much since Bobby died. It didn't seem to matter to his parents that they still had him...all they ever thought about was Bobby! Mike was feeling terrible.

Facts about the Feelings of Grief

Mike is Bobby's older brother and feels guilty that he wasn't able to keep Bobby from being killed. He also feels guilty about the times he didn't like having a younger brother and wished he'd go away. This is normal. Most brothers and sisters feel that way at times. Mike is confused by his many feelings. He is also confused about the different feelings of others in his family.

Mike's parents may feel unable to control their crying and sadness, and they are frightened. They worry about how to protect Mike and keep him safe. Anger sometimes comes out when people try to feel powerful and in control. People often wear a mask of one feeling to keep a different feeling inside. The way people look or act may not be the way they are really feeling. You might feel as if there is a wall between you when that happens.

Kristy is a young child, and she is more likely to show her sadness through her behavior. She may act noisy or naughty, become more fearful, and have nightmares because of family changes.

When families lose a member they love, they all grieve, each in their own way and in their own time. It is difficult to see people you love grieving. You can't take their pain away, and you can't fix it. No one can take your pain away, either.

The grief process

Grief is a natural reaction to loss. It is called a process because it doesn't happen all at once, but gradually, and many people experience a similar pattern of feelings. In general, grief can be divided into three phases or parts.

1. Shock and denial

At first a loss does not seem real. Shock is nature's way of protecting people until they are able to adjust to difficult events. When you're in shock, you can do what needs to be done, but you don't really understand what happened, and you don't feel anything. Shock usually passes quickly, but **denial** can last a long time.

It is natural to try to avoid painful feelings. Part of you knows you will never see the person who died ever again. Another part of you doesn't want to believe it— you *deny* what has happened. You may try to keep busy doing other things to not think about it. You may feel embarrassed and want to pretend nothing has changed.

2. Confusion and despair

It isn't easy to learn how to cope with strong and painful feelings. You may fear the unknown and want to get back what you lost. You often feel helpless and hopeless when you know you can't.

You may feel angry at yourself or blame someone else. Most people will feel opposite feelings at the same time. You might feel angry at the people you love, for example. You may feel very lonely and think no one cares about you. You may search for reasons when there are no reasons—terrible things just happen sometimes.

You may hope for things to happen that you know can't happen. You may see or hear things you don't think you can hear or see. You may wonder if you are going crazy. You aren't.

3. Eventually acceptance will come

The third phase begins when you learn to adjust to the world without the person you lost. You may always feel some sadness, but the unbearable pain will end.

There will be times when sadness comes back like waves in the ocean. The feeling will be powerful at times, and a gentle reminder at other times.

Going through these phases of grief is hard, but the experience helps you become a stronger person and more understanding of others. You will learn you can cope with difficult times. You will know who and what is important to you, perhaps. In time, you will be able to love yourself and others again. The world will seem real and worthwhile again.

Feelings are all okay!

Feelings are what make us human. Feeling something is different from *knowing* something. Feelings are just as important as facts, however, because they affect what you do. Close your eyes and think of a time when you felt very angry. Where do you feel anger in your body? Think of a time when you felt very sad. Where do you feel sadness in your body?

When you were very young, you probably felt anger in your hands and feet, and you wanted to punch and kick. When you learned you couldn't do this, your feelings may have moved inward. When you keep feelings stuffed inside, they can cause pain, such as headaches or stomachaches. You may feel as if your heart will break, if that is where you hold your sadness.

It is normal and natural to have all kinds of feelings. Everyone reacts to feelings in different ways. When someone dies, your feelings may be frightening because they are new and seem powerful. It is important to learn something about the many kinds of feelings you might have when someone you love dies.

Fear—Suddenly the world seems unsafe and out of control. That is scary! Most people begin to worry about themselves and others dying after someone they love dies. You may wonder what would happen to you if your parents died. Someone would love you and take care of you. It is all right to ask who that would be.

Anger—Most people feel some anger when someone dies. They may feel angry at the doctor, the church, God, or anyone they think caused the death or didn't prevent it from happening. It is all right to feel angry. Anger is a natural feeling. Anger must be released in a way that doesn't hurt anything or anyone, though. Anger can be a problem if it turns into rage or hate.

Jealousy—Most people feel jealous when they see someone enjoying something they do not have. After you've experienced the death of someone close, it can seem as if other people have perfect lives or perfect families. But everyone has problems and difficult times.

Depression—There are times when people feel empty, helpless, and even hopeless. Life doesn't seem to have any meaning, and it is difficult to do anything. These periods of despair are referred to as **depression**. Depression can be serious, and if people are unable to sleep or eat because of it, they need to see a doctor.

Rejection—It is easy to feel punished and abandoned when someone dies. People might think God doesn't love them enough to protect them from pain and loss. They wonder if the person who died didn't love them enough to keep on living. They begin to feel no one loves them!

Guilt—People often feel guilty and wonder if something they did or thought when they were angry caused the death. Thoughts and wishes cannot cause death. No one is perfect. Everyone has something they wish they had or hadn't done.

Sometimes death comes after a long illness, and a survivor feels glad about the death instead of sad. It is all right to welcome the end of something terrible. Sadness may come later.

Feelings change

A feeling is your body's signal of how you are reacting to something. You cannot tell yourself how to feel. Feelings cannot be changed because someone else tells you to. Difficult feelings may not change quickly. It is important to learn how to let your feelings out so they don't cause physical or mental problems.

5
Letting out Your Feelings

"This is a difficult time for all of us," Ms. Wilson said sadly to the 6th-grade class. She looked at the empty desk in the third row. Yesterday she had placed a white rose in a vase there when she told the class about Jane's death from congenital heart failure.

"She was only her teacher," Sarah thought. Her eyes

avoided both Ms. Wilson and the empty desk across the aisle. "Jane was my friend! I can't believe she's really dead." Sarah looked up at Ms. Wilson and saw the sadness in her face. Sarah looked around the room and knew that most of the class felt terrible, too.

"I'd like to do something special today," Ms. Wilson said, passing out sheets of paper. "We are all thinking about Jane today. I'd like you to try to put some of your memories of her on paper, in words or pictures."

"Oh, no!" Sarah thought, holding back tears. "I don't want to think about her. I didn't even want to come to school today."

Sarah had been very quiet since she heard the news. Her father had tried to comfort her. "Congenital heart disease means she was born with a faulty heart. It wasn't strong like yours and mine." But Sarah wouldn't talk anymore about it.

Her parents had decided it was important for her to be with her classmates today. Her father tried to cheer Sarah up with a nice breakfast. He didn't know how frightened and sad Sarah felt inside.

"Why Jane?" Sarah thought only old people had heart attacks. "She was young."

In school, Sarah looked at the blank sheet of paper in front of her. "Jane is dead, and I can't stop worrying about myself and my parents, wondering if we could die."

She decided she'd rather think about the fun times she and Jane had had. She remembered the treasure hunt they planned for Jane's little brother. Sarah drew a map on the paper, and their houses. She felt guilty about some of the things she'd said when they got mad at each other.

Sarah looked back at Scott. He was writing a poem. She wondered how he felt. He had been Jane's boyfriend, until he found someone he liked better!

"Jane and I used to tell each other everything," Sarah smiled as she thought about some of their secrets. She couldn't put those on paper, but she drew a book and wrote "secrets" on it. She drew a cloud and painted "dreams." She circled it all with a large heart.

"This isn't a great picture," she thought. "But I enjoyed doing it, and I feel like talking about Jane now."

"Let's talk for a while about your memories of Jane." Ms. Wilson stood up with her own sheet of paper. "I'd like to begin . . . and when we finish, we'll write a note to Jane's family to let them know we share their sorrow."

Facts about Expressing Grief

Sarah misses her friend and worries about others dying. She is embarrassed about her fears and doesn't want to talk about them until she realizes that others feel bad also. Her teacher will help the members of the class understand and express their feelings.

After a friend or relative dies, many people worry that someone else will die. Some people begin to worry about everyone and everything important to them. Almost everyone worries a little bit about themselves. Headaches and stomachaches are often signals of difficult feelings kept inside. Keeping feelings inside can cause sleeping and eating problems, too.

Everyone needs someone to talk to

All feelings are okay. It is all right to tell someone that you are afraid or worried. Sometimes, just talking about these things makes you feel better. Maybe you need more information and the person you talk to will tell you what you need to know.

It is important to decide who you want to talk to. Some people are uncomfortable talking about serious things. They want everything to be fun, and they laugh and tease you to get you to think of other, less serious things. Others feel bad when they can't fix things and make everything all right. Some things can't be fixed.

Your school counselor may be able to help you find a grief **support group**, where you can talk with others who have experienced a death.

Memories to keep and memories to let go

No one remembers everything that happens to her or him. Some things are easily forgotten. Looking at pictures and talking about things is a way to keep good memories alive. Photographs, drawings, poems, and stories can be kept in a book to help remember special people and good times.

Some events are very painful, and you may try to put them out of your mind. But you may lose the happy memories along with the bad. Most people discover they need to talk about the difficult times with someone. The difficult memories become less painful then, and it is easier to remember the happier times.

Moving your feelings

Sports, exercise, dance, and other forms of movement are good ways to express anger naturally. Kicking a football, hitting a tennis ball, or running are all good things to do when you feel angry. Depression is sometimes caused by anger turned in at yourself. Exercise can help you feel better.

Expressing feelings creatively

Music can help you release all kinds of feelings. Playing an instrument or records or tapes can be very healing. Many people let out feelings by screaming. It may feel good to scream, but it's usually unpleasant or frightening to others. Try screaming into a pillow. You can also let your feelings out by singing.

Writing is a good way to express thoughts and feelings. You can put things you want to say, but feel unable to, in a letter that will never be mailed. A journal or diary is also a safe place to write about your powerful feelings. The journal accepts whatever you write without teasing you or putting you down.

Creating art or just doodling is another good way to express feelings. Shapes, lines, and colors can be used to express a wide range of feelings. You can express angry rage without hurting anyone by scribbling furiously with a red crayon on an old newspaper. You can take the power away from a nightmare or a terrible event by drawing it out on paper. Happy memories can be drawn, framed, and kept forever.

GUIDELINES FOR CREATIVE GRIEF WORK

CREATE A GRIEF JOURNAL

1) Buy a simple three-ring or spiral notebook.
2) Choose a comfortable pen that pleases you.
3) Keep colored pencils, paint, or crayons available to express thoughts and feelings that you cannot express in words.
4) Make time to write each day.
5) Write in a quiet place, or play soft music in the background.
6) Don't worry about spelling, punctuation, or sentence structure.
7) Express your thoughts and feelings honestly.
8) Keep your journal in a safe place, just for you.
9) Reread your journal from time to time to be aware of changes in your behavior and feelings.

EXPRESS YOURSELF IN POETRY

1) Rhyming isn't necessary. A poem can be a few carefully chosen words arranged in a pleasing form.
2) A lyric poem is one that expresses intense personal emotions.
3) Haiku is a poetic form from Japan. It has three lines, with five syllables in the first line, seven in the second, and five in the third. To create a haiku, use simple words that express a strong feeling and create a vivid image.

EXPERIMENT WITH ART

1) Allow your inner child to mourn. Use lines, colors, and shapes to express thoughts and feelings too difficult for words.
2) Use a red crayon to scribble and release anger.
3) Use soft blue crayons or watercolors to release sadness.
4) Draw your fears to conquer them.
5) Draw or paint something you enjoy to give yourself a sense of control.

6
When a Family Member Dies

Lisa closed her math book and pushed it aside. "I wish Mom would get home from work," she thought. It was the first week of school and it was hard to think about homework.

"School is the pits this year," she said to herself. "Last year was hard because Dad was so sick with cancer. It's even worse since he died. Everything is different." They had moved from their house to an apartment last month.

"There's no one here after school." Lisa felt lonely. Her brother would come home later, and it seemed like a long time before her mother would be home from work. Lisa remembered happier times in the other house with the whole family. She also remembered sad times.

"Who are all these people?" she had asked her

brother after the funeral. There were too many strangers in the house. "Why are they here?"

"You know some of them," he had told her. "They're neighbors or friends of Mom and Dad." Lisa hadn't recognized many. They had looked sad and some had been crying. She didn't like to see adults cry.

"I just wish they would take their hams and turkeys and go home," Lisa thought to herself. "Our refrigerator is stuffed with food." Lisa wanted to be alone with her mother. She wanted Mom to hold her and tell her everything would be all right. She had been embarrassed at school. It seemed like everyone was looking at her and feeling sorry for her.

Most of the people at the funeral had avoided talking to Lisa, except for one man. He owned the company where her dad had worked. He had told her he would never find anyone as good as her dad.

"Neither will I," Lisa thought. She wondered if her mom would start dating, like some widowed mothers did. "I'd hate that. I wouldn't want her to ever get married again."

Lisa watched a car turn in the driveway down the street. A man got out and walked over to hug his little boy. Lisa felt jealous when she saw other kids with a father. She was starting to stay away from her friends' houses where there were two parents.

Lisa went back to her books. "Mom should be home by now," she worried. "What if something happened to her!" Lisa often wondered who would take care of her if her mom died. Her brother was only 16 and she knew they couldn't live alone. Mom got angry at her and her brother when they argued about jobs around the house. "I need more help around here," she had shouted at him last week. It seemed to Lisa that her mother was always getting angry about little things, but she didn't even notice some big problems.

"Mom's different. She changed when Dad died," Lisa had told her grampa. He hadn't said much. He seemed different too. He missed his son. Sometimes it seemed to Lisa that everyone she loved had gone away.

Facts about the Death of a Family Member

Lisa is feeling pretty discouraged. She's worried about herself and others. The death of a parent can create many changes in a family. Lisa probably thinks she will never be happy again. Her life will never be the same, but she will have happy times again.

Grieving families

Families are people who live together. Families help and support each other, and every person plays a part in a family. When one person dies, you miss what they did for you and what you did for them. You miss what they meant to you. That might be love, companionship, security, or even someone to fight with! It takes a while for the family to work well together again.

Members of families grieve differently because they have different losses. When you are very young, you need your parents to survive. As you get older and develop some independence, you need your parents in other ways. Adults can manage on their own, but they still grieve when their parents die, because they lose an important part of their past. The elderly grieve the death of an adult child because they expect their children to live longer than them.

Families who have experienced a death may fight more because of stress. Parents and children may become very protective of each other. The person who died may be remembered as more perfect than anyone can really be. No one can replace another person, but some people may try.

Death of a parent

When one of your parents dies, you lose an important feeling of security. It is natural to worry about the other parent, because you need him or her so much. The surviving parent may seem different and unable to give you the comfort you need because of his or her own loss and grief.

You may find it hard to see adults cry, but they need to cry to grieve. Tears can help reduce stress. Most people feel better after they cry. Many adults try to hide their sadness from their children, but it is better if they cry together.

The death of one parent leaves the other with a lot of extra work. You may be asked to help more than before. You will feel important because you are needed. You must be careful not to take on adult tasks or grow up too fast, though. You can't take your mother's or father's place.

Family times

Times that are supposed to be happy may seem especially sad after the death of a family member. Holidays, birthdays, and other family celebrations are difficult after a death. You can plan to do something special on those days. It helps to talk about the person who died and share feelings and memories. Perhaps you can think of something special to honor the person's memory.

FINDING GRIEF SUPPORT

List family members you can share concerns and feelings:

_____

_____

_____

List friends you can share your concerns and feelings:

_____

_____

_____

List others you can go to for support:

When and where do you feel OK about crying?

7
When Someone Else Is Grieving

The apartment complex where Tracy lived was on a busy street, so the scream of the siren was a familiar sound. She didn't think much about it until the siren blocked out all other sounds, then suddenly stopped.

"That's right here," Tracy thought as she hurried to the window. A rescue squad had stopped outside her building.

"Tanya!" she called to her cousin in the next room. Tanya came over every afternoon to help out while Tracy's mom was at work. Tanya was getting her two-year-old son dressed after his nap when Tracy called.

"Let's find out what happened," Tanya said. She propped her son on one hip and opened the door.

Two men in uniform rushed past them toward the end of the hall, where a woman was calling to them from her open door.

"Hurry! It's his heart again!" Tracy recognized the woman as Mrs. Edwards.

"Oh, no," Tracy gasped. Mrs. Edwards was her friend Angela's mother.

Tracy and Tanya went outside and joined the curious crowd that had gathered. Tracy looked for a familiar face and wondered where Angela was.

"He had a heart attack last spring," an older woman reported to the man next to her. "He can't survive another."

Three boys came racing around the corner on their bikes. "Did someone get shot?" they asked Tracy. She didn't want to talk to them.

"Clear the way," a police officer ordered. "We need to get through here."

"Let's go back inside." Tanya took Tracy's arm. "We're just in the way here."

The hall looked twice as long and extra dark when they were inside. It was very quiet.

"I'm scared," Tracy said when they were in their apartment. "What can we do?"

"Nothing right now. We have to wait until your mother comes home. She'll know what to do." Tanya put her arm around Tracy.

Someone was knocking loudly on the door. "That must be her now," Tanya said. But it was Mrs. Edwards standing there when Tanya opened the door. Mrs. Edwards's eyes were wide and full of tears.

"They say he's dead! I don't believe it. I'm going to the hospital. Could you stay with Angela for a while?"

"Of course," Tanya answered. "We'll go right now." She took her son's hand and started toward the door. Tracy didn't follow.

"I'll come later when Mom gets home." Tracy watched them leave. She felt very alone, but she was afraid to go see her friend. She didn't know what to say or do.

In a few minutes her mother came home. She had heard about Mr. Edwards. "These things happen," she told Tracy. She held Tracy in her arms and they both cried. "He was a good man," Tracy's mother said. "We'll have to do what we can to help the family. I made a big kettle of soup last night. We'll take that over there."

"Do we have to go now?" Tracy's jaw tightened.

"Yes, honey. People need friends during times like this. Angela is your friend."

"But what if she's crying? I won't know how to make her feel better." Tracy held back. "I won't know what to say."

"You can't make her feel differently," her mother began. "You can only tell her that you are sorry about what happened. You can even tell her you are scared and don't know what to say. If you are honest, maybe she will be able to tell you how she really feels, too. She just needs someone to listen to her."

"What if she doesn't say anything?" Tracy asked. She was beginning to feel better about going.

"That's all right. She might prefer to watch television or play a game. You don't have to treat her differently. We just need to let her and her family know that we care."

Helping Others When Someone They Love Dies

Most people wonder what they can do to help when there is a death or crisis. Tanya was wise to suggest they go inside and stay out of the way. She was willing to help where she was needed, too.

Recognize your own feelings

Tracy felt afraid when her friend's parent died. Death does not seem like a threat until someone you know dies. Most people feel anxious and uncomfortable.

Do you avoid being around people who have had someone die? You can't "catch" death. Your friend or relative usually needs your support and caring. It may be hard to go to their house the first time after the death.

Letting others know you care

Go to the funeral to let your friend and his or her family know you care and want to be with them. You don't have to say anything special.

Send cards or letters to let them know you are thinking about them. Take gifts of flowers or food or anything that lets them know you care. They may get many calls and cards the first month and very few after that. They need to be remembered longer. Grief lasts longer than a few weeks. It won't last forever, but it lasts a long time.

Accepting your friend's grief

Your friend may or may not act differently after experiencing the death of a loved one. It's all right for your friend to be more serious and not as much fun for a while.

Accept the person's feelings. All feelings are okay and need to be expressed in some way. His or her feelings will change. You don't need to cheer your friend up.

Share your own feelings of sadness with your friend if the person who died was someone you knew. Let your friend know how much you care about him or her.

Try to be a good listener. This is what your friend needs most. Talking about the death helps people accept what happened. You don't have to fix it for them.

THINKING

Thinking back on memories I hold so dear,
  I see my visions fading as I add on the years.
Crying through the hard times, smiling through the good,
  Holding on to memories is all that I can do.
Think of life all over, omitting all the bad,
  I try to remember someone by reaching out my hands.
Someone grab my hands and hold them tight.
  I need love so much right now.
  Someone show me light.

- Joanna Redman, age twelve

8
Feeling Good about You

Mike was furious when his mother told him about the grief support group.

"I'm not going! You can't make me go!" he screamed at his mother. "Why me?" he thought. "Why did this happen to me?" He didn't want to go to one more place that would remind him about his little brother Bobby and how he died.

"Just once," his mother urged him. "If you don't want to go again, you won't have to."

When Mike arrived at the group, six other kids about his age were there. He didn't expect to like the group, but it was okay. No one cried. They didn't *have* to talk, but everyone did. They learned to use pictures to tell a story. Before Mike knew it, it was almost time to leave.

"Today we talked about loss and change and why you are here," Mrs. Jordon said as she collected their drawings. "I'd like to know how you feel about our group, and if you want to come again."

"I liked it!" Jason spoke up. "I liked drawing pictures. We don't get to do that in school very often. It was fun."

"Well," Mike looked embarrassed, "I didn't want to come here at all. I didn't know what a grief group was. My mom made me come. It was okay though...I'll come again next week."

Ann helped pick up the cups and napkins left over from the treats they had. "I thought I was the only one around here that had someone die. I felt weird and really different. But now I see I'm not the only one. I feel better already."

"We'll meet six times," Mrs. Jordon told them. "We'll talk about death and funerals next time. You will also learn about the many feelings of grief. I think you'll find out that this is a place where you can talk about the things that worry you."

"I can tell you right now that I'm worried that my

mom will forget to pick me up!" Ann complained. "She forgets everything."

"I'm sure she'll come." Mrs. Jordon smiled. "And you will learn how to take better care of yourself, too."

Taking Care of Yourself

Lisa, Sarah, Mike, and Ann met each other in a grief support group. They learned it was a good place to go to talk about their feelings and problems. It helped them feel good about themselves.

Feeling different

Even though many people love and care for you, there will be times you feel all alone. This may happen when there are many people around you. You feel different from them because your problems are different.

You may feel different because everyone else in your family feels very sad all the time—and you don't. Maybe your life hasn't changed as much as some of the other family members'. Maybe you will grieve when you get older.

Grieving is something you have to do in your own way in your own time. Reading a book like this can help you accept yourself.

Difficult times

You may get telephone calls for the person who died and not know what to say. You can say the person has died, or you can say, "Only my father lives here," or "Only my mother lives here now."

Filling out forms that ask the name of your father and mother are painful reminders, if one of them has died. You write "dead" or "not living" instead of their name. You will often be asked the same questions over and over about when and how your parent died. It gets easier. Sometimes you wish everyone knew, and sometimes you wish they didn't.

You will also be asked how many brothers and sisters you have. If one of them died, you wonder if you should include that one. You can say the number living.

Some people think they see or feel the presence of the person who died. Some are comforted by this and others are frightened. People will not think you are crazy if you talk about it. There are mysteries in both life and death that we have no answers for.

Problems at school

You may feel embarrassed to return to school after a death in the family, because you feel different. While you are gone, your teacher will explain to the class what happened. Friends don't know what to say, and you sense their concern. It is all right to talk about death. Many people don't know that.

There may be times at school when you feel like crying. You may worry that your friends will call you a baby if you cry. It is all right to cry when you feel sad. You can talk to your teacher or school nurse about leaving the room when you need to if you would rather do that.

There may be times when it will be difficult to do

your schoolwork. You may be worried about someone at home or have other worries. It is important that your teachers know about the death, even several years later. It may affect your schoolwork for a long time, but you can get extra help.

Stress and relaxation

Death creates changes, and changes lead to stress. Stress is a feeling of tension that happens when your body adjusts to a difficult experience. There are some things you can do to lower stress and to feel better about yourself. (See box on page 59.)

Support systems

You need all kinds of support when someone dies, because grief can be one of the most painful things you will ever feel. Because members of a family have to deal with their own feelings of grief, they often find it difficult to help each other through the pain. You can't always rely on family members for support.

Some families have many relatives and friends who are able to help them manage the changes in their lives. There are also many grief support groups for adults in churches, synagogues, hospitals, and community centers. Sometimes they offer groups for children. Your school may have a grief support group, or the school counselor can help you find one in your community.

If your parent or brother or sister has died, you may need individual **counseling** by someone trained to understand and talk with children. It helps to have a place to share feelings with someone who understands. If you have a friend who is willing to listen, you can also talk about the death with your friend.

Healing

The day will come when the world seems all right to you again. You will feel safe and secure and enjoy the people around you. If you have grieved, you will be more patient and understand yourself and others better. You will appreciate people and life more. You will be a stronger person because of the pain you have had the courage to face.

Avoiding stress

- Eat at regular times even though you may not feel very hungry. Avoid junk food such as candy, cookies, potato chips, and fast food.

- Get a good night's sleep. A glass of milk before you go to bed might help you relax. Soft drinks with caffeine, tea, and chocolate could all make it harder to fall asleep.

- Make time for plenty of exercise. You will have more energy and feel better. Try to spend time doing activities you enjoy, such as biking, walking outside, and playing sports.

- Try not to worry about the future. Imagine good things happening to you.

- When you have feelings of panic or fear, take long deep breaths and breathe out slowly.

- Remember that it's okay to feel sad. Don't try to make yourself feel cheerful if that's not how you're feeling.

Glossary

cancer—an uncontrolled growth of cells somewhere in the body

casket—a box or chest used to bury a dead body; another word used for this box is *coffin*

congenital—a disease or condition you are born with

corpse—a dead body

counseling—talking with a person who is trained to help others with their problems

cremate—to reduce to ashes by burning

deceased—dead

denial—refusing to admit that something is true or has happened

depression—periods of despair or sadness, sometimes marked by lack of activity

embalming—a process that replaces the blood in the veins of the **corpse** with a fluid that will preserve the body

funeral—ritual held to mourn a dead person before burial

grave—a hole in the earth in which a body is buried

grief—the many feelings you feel when you lose something or someone very important to you

heart attack—when the walls or arteries of the heart become plugged and the heart stops beating

hereditary—something you inherit from a parent or grandparent or other ancestor

life cycle—the series of stages that a living creature passes through during its lifetime

life span— the length of the life of a living creature

mortician—a person who prepares a dead person for burial; another word that means the same thing is *undertaker*

stroke—a sudden loss of brain function, which happens when blood is blocked from reaching the brain

suicide—when someone ends his or her own life

support group—a gathering of people who meet to help each other deal with a problem or situation

taps—a bugle call blown at military funerals

wake—a time for people to see a dead person before he or she is buried

The Drawing Out Feelings Series

This new series designed by Marge Heegaard provides parents and professionals with an organized approach to helping children ages 6-12 cope with feelings resulting from family loss and change.

Designed to be used in an adult/child setting, these workbooks provide age-appropriate educational concepts and questions to help children identify and accept their feelings. Children are given the opportunity to work out their emotions during difficult times while learning to recognize acceptable behavior, and conflicts can be resolved and self-esteem increased while the coping skills for loss and change are being developed.

All four titles are formatted so that children can easily illustrate their answers to the important questions in the text.

Leaders Guide

Facilitator Guide For
DRAWING OUT FEELINGS

Structure and suggestions for
helping children, individually
or in groups, cope with feelings
from family change. Includes
directions for six organized
sessions for each of the four
workbooks.
114 pp. 8½x11 ISBN 0-9620502-5-3
$30.00

When Someone Very Special Dies
Children Can Learn to Cope with Grief

A workbook to help children deal with their feelings about death.

Here is a practical format for allowing children to understand the concept of death and develop coping skills for life. Children, with adult supervision, are invited to illustrate and personalize their loss through art. This workbook encourages the child to identify support systems and personal strengths. "I especially appreciate the design of this book...the child becomes an active participant in

pictorially and verbally doing something about [their loss]." —Dean J. Hempel, M.D., Child Psychiatrist
Grief/Psychology/Parenting
Ages 6–12
36 pp, 11 x 8 1/2", $9.95
trade paperback
ISBN 0-9620502-0-2

When Someone Has a Very Serious Illness

A workbook to help children deal with their feelings about serious illness.

An excellent resource for helping children learn the basic concepts of illness and various age-appropriate ways of coping with someone else's illness. "...offers children a positive tool for coping with those many changes." —Christine Ternand, M.D., Pediatrician

Health/Grief/Psychology
Ages 6–12, 41 pp, 11 x 8 1/2", $9.95
trade paperback, ISBN 0-9620502-4-5

When Something Terrible Happens

A workbook to help children deal with their feelings about traumatic events.

Empowers children to explore feelings, and reduces nightmares and post-traumatic stress symptoms. "This healing book...combines story, pictures, information, and art therapy in a way that appeals to children." —Stephanie Frogge, Director of Victim Outreach, M.A.D.D.

Grief/Psychology/Parenting
Ages 6-12, 36 pp, 11x8 1/2", $9.95
trade paperback, ISBN 0-9620502-3-7

When Mom and Dad Separate

A workbook to help children deal with their feelings about separation/divorce.

This bestselling workbook helps youngsters discuss the basic concepts of marriage and divorce, allowing them to work through all the powerful and confusing feelings resulting from their parents' decision to separate.

Divorce/Grief/Psychology
Ages 6-12, 36 pp, 11x8 1/2", $9.95
trade paperback, ISBN 0-9620502-2-9

Marge Eaton Heegaard, MA, is a licensed clinical social worker and art therapist. Author of the DRAWING OUT FEELING SERIES and the DRAWING TOGETHER SERIES, Heegaard has been a leader in using the art process to help adults and children express feelings of grief from loss and change. Her books are enjoyed and recommended by parents, educators, counselors, social workers, clergy, physicians and other professionals. She lives in Minneapolis, MN.

When a Family Is In Trouble
Children Can Cope With Grief From Drug and Alcohol Addictions

A workbook to help children through the trauma of a parent's chemical dependency problem.

This helpful workbook provides basic information about addictions and encourages healthy coping skills. Children express personal trauma and feelings more easily in pictures than in words, and the pages of this title are perfect to "draw out" those feelings and hurts. There is plenty of room for a child's artwork.

Ages 6–12
36 pp, 11 x 8 1/2", $9.95
trade paperback
ISBN 0-9620502-7-X

NEW

GROWING UP...
AND GRIEVING

Life in middle school is defined by change. This book begins with changes in everyday life before focusing on grief from the death of a loved one. Creativity is encouraged to help them understand and express feelings needed to cope with grief.

AGES 10-14   70 pp. 5 1/2 x 8 ½ $9.95
Trade paperback, ISBN 13 9780996639019

WOODLAND PRESS
952-830-9423
marheeg@me.com

PLEASE NOTE AND FILE FOR FUTURE ORDERS

For orders less than 12 copies please contact your local bookstore or order online searching by title

National Book Network will now be fulfilling all quantity orders for WOODLAND PRESS at the same or better discounts. For ordering details please contact:

Sylvia Williams
National Book Network
4501 Forbes Blvd.
Suite 200
Lanham, MD 20706
301-459-3366 ext. 5523
swilliams@nbnbooks.com

NEW!
GRIEVING AND GROWING: Developing and Leading Teen Or Adult Grief Support Groups
Begin with a small group for Teens in schools or colleges or adults in any setting...or develop a large coalition of community resources for grief support. Churches, Hospitals, Hospices, Funeral Homes, Counselors and other professionals can work together to develop weekly grief groups.. Speaker topics, educational handouts and facilitator training program is included.

$35.00 PBK * 8 ½ x 11 * 115 pages
ISBN 13 978-09966390-0-2

The DRAWING TOGETHER SERIES
To Increase Learning And Communication Between Children And Adults

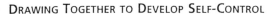

DRAWING TOGETHER TO LEARN ABOUT FEELINGS

MARGE EATON HEEGAARD

This art therapy book helps children understand feelings and the proper way to express them, learn to be sensitive to the feelings of others, and develop coping skills for the difficult times in their lives. Adults can use the book to see how children express in pictures what they are unable to say in words.

ISBN: 1-57749-136-X • $9.95 PBK • 8 ¹/₂ X 11 • 40 PAGES

DRAWING TOGETHER TO DEVELOP SELF-CONTROL

MARGE EATON HEEGAARD

An art therapy book for children with controllable behavioral problems. Kids will learn the consequences of their actions, how their misbehavior affects others, how to develop good judgment skills, and more.

ISBN: 1-57749-101-7 • $9.95 PBK • 8 ¹/₂ X 11 • 40 PAGES

DRAWING TOGETHER TO MANAGE ANGER

MARGE EATON HEEGAARD

This art therapy book helps children understand anger and find appropriate ways to express unhappiness, develop effective conflict resolutions skills, and learn how to better cope with disappointment and frustration. Adults can use the book to see how children express in pictures what they are unable to say in words.

ISBN: 1-57749-137-8 • $9.95 PBK • 8 ¹/₂ X 11 • 48 PAGES

DRAWING TOGETHER TO ACCEPT AND RESPECT DIFFERENCES

MARGE EATON HEEGAARD

This art therapy book helps children cherish their own unique qualities; respect other races, religions, cultures, opinions, and lifestyles; be sensitive to others' disabilities; overcome feelings of helplessness or isolation; and stand up for themselves and others. Adults can use the book to see how children express in pictures what they are unable to say in words. The completed book becomes a keepsake of an important period in the child's life.

ISBN: 1-57749-138-6 • $9.95 PBK • 8 ¹/₂ X 11 • 40 PAGES

DRAWING TOGETHER TO BUILD CHARACTER

MARGE EATON HEEGAARD

This art therapy book helps children learn and display the important character values of kindness, respectfulness, responsibility, honesty, fairness, and gratitude. Adults can use the book to see how children express in pictures what they are unable to say in words. The completed book becomes a keepsake of an important period in the child's life.

ISBN: 1-57749-148-3 • $9.95 PBK • 8 ¹/₂ X 11 • 40 PAGES

The DRAWING OUT FEELINGS SERIES
To help Children Cope With Loss And Change
by Marge Heegaard

LIVING WELL WITH MY SERIOUS ILLNESS

An art therapy book for helping children cope with the early stages of a serious illness. Sensitive exercises address the questions children have during this emotional and troubling crisis. Children are encouraged to express in pictures what they are often incapable of expressing in words.

ISBN: 1-57749-139-4 • $9.95 PBK • 10¹/₄ X 8¹/₂ • 40 PAGES • AVAILABLE 11/03

CUANDO ALGUIEN MUY ESPECIAL MUERE
LOS NIÑOS PUEDEN APRENDER A ENFRENTAR LA ADVERSIDAD

Introducing the Spanish edition of *When Someone Very Special Dies*, the world's bestselling art therapy book for grieving children. This book was designed to teach basic concepts of death and help children understand and express the many feelings they have when someone very special dies. Communication is increased and coping skills are developed as children illustrate their books with their personal stories.

ISBN: 1-57749-127-0 • $9.95 PBK • 10¹/₄ X 8¹/₂ • 40 PAGES

BEYOND THE RAINBOW
A WORKBOOK FOR CHILDREN IN THE ADVANCED STAGES OF A VERY SERIOUS ILLNESS

Through the creative and interactive drawing activities in this book, kids can learn to communicate openly about their life-threatening illness, overcome fear and anxiety, develop important coping skills, discuss concerns about their treatment, share thoughts and feelings about death, express difficult feelings in appropriate ways, regain a sense of power in their lives, communicate personal wishes, and maintain hope.

ISBN: 1-57749-129-7 • $9.95 PBK • 10¹/₄ X 8¹/₂ • 40 PAGES

SAYING GOODBYE TO YOUR PET
CHILDREN CAN LEARN TO COPE WITH PET LOSS

An art therapy book for children coping with the loss of a pet. Sensitive exercises help children say in pictures what they are unable to say in words. The completed book serves as a lasting keepsake, honoring the memory of the family pet and its importance in the child's life.

ISBN: 1-57749-106-8 • $9.95 PBK • 10¹/₄ X 8¹/₂ • 40 PAGES

When Adults Hurt Children
Helping Children Heal from Abuse
by Marge Eaton Heegaard

Book Description: Child abuse is any mistreatment or neglect that causes harm or injury to a child. This book is written to help children heal from abuse. When facilitated by a trained adult, its creative and interactive drawing activities can help children cope with the emotional aftermath of abuse

ISBN: 1-57749-152-1 • $9.95 PBK • 10¹/₄ X 8¹/₂ • 32 PAGES

Adopted and Wondering
Drawing Out Feelings
Marge Eaton Heegaard

Adoption is a life-altering event—a change that can create loss and grief as well as joy. If the feelings created by change are not addressed, children can develop problems with identity, trust, control, self-esteem, and intimacy. This book uses the art process to help children understand and express their feelings about being adopted

ISBN 978-1-57749-166-8 • $9.95 • 8-1/2 x 11 • 40 pp